© 2009 Greater Impact Ministries, Inc. All rights reserved. No portion of this book may be reproduced, stored in a retrieval system, or transmitted in any form or by any means – electronic, mechanical, photocopy, recording, or any other – except for brief quotations in printed reviews, without the prior permission of the publisher.

Scriptures are taken from the following: The Holy Bible, New International Version. Copyright © 1973, 1978, 1984, International Bible Society. Used by permission of Zondervan Bible Publishers. The Holy Bible, New Living Translation®. Copyright © 1996. Used by permission of Tyndale House Publishers, Inc., Wheaton, Illinois 60189. All rights reserved. The New American Standard Bible®. Copyright © 1960, 1962, 1963, 1968, 1971, 1972,1973,1975, 1995 by The Lockman Foundation. Used by permission. The King James Version of the Bible. Public domain. The New King James Version®. Copyright © 1982 by Thomas Nelson, Inc. Used by permission. All rights reserved. The Message by Eugene H. Peterson. Copyright © 1993, 1994, 1995, 1996, 2000, 2001, 2002. Used by permission of NavPress Publishing Group. All rights reserved.

Printed in the United States of America, Greater Impact Ministries, Inc., 554 Belle Meade Farm Drive, Loveland, OH 45140.

Much appreciation is shown to God for His inspiration, and Debbie Hitchcock and Nina Roesner for their collective vision.

May we all continue to honor Him in what we do.

May your soul as a wife be filled as you spend time with Him each week in preparation for Daughters of Sarah®.

It is our prayer that this intentional time with Him becomes a life-long habit that blesses you in ways nothing else ever will.

Thank you for choosing to take the journey with us!

How to use *The Redeeming Work Journal* with *Daughters of Sarah*

Welcome to *Daughters of Sarah* and *The Redeeming Work Journal*!

Nina asked me to write the introduction to the journal because she knows I happen to be a person who loves to journal, and I'm sure many of you are, too. While I'm confident not everyone holding this book is piping with enthusiasm, I realize some are.

For many of you, just holding this book is overwhelming, and it looks daunting! *"What am I supposed to do with all those blank lines?" "Where are the questions to answer?"* **First of all, let me assure you that there is *no wrong way* to begin the process.** Hopefully, it will all make sense—if you will bear with me for a few minutes—while I share my story.

My Story

As part of the second Daughters of Sarah Class in 2006, I saw all the class materials in a clunky, three-inch, loose-leaf binder that included everything you will now find in the *Daughters of Sarah Participant Manual* and *The Redeeming Work Journal*. Carrying the manual around was one thing, but putting it in my lap to do homework was quite another. I could hardly write in it—physically—as I curled up to spend time with God trying to work through the materials. It was just too big!

For me, class homework was one thing. I could easily fill in the blanks, write out my stories, and think through the answers to questions. But spending time with God and asking him to peel back the blinders that were impacting my marriage, my kids, and my other relationships was where I wanted to focus: on the scriptures! I desired to take the scriptures from the course and weave them into the fabric of my soul, so that I could reflect His Glory! In order to do that, I put all the scripture verses in a separate journal with my thoughts and reflections, in one place and a manner that would allow me to use it virtually anywhere.

Through many revisions of the *Daughters of Sarah Participant Manual*, Nina and I found it fitting to put all the scriptures into a journal format like I had originally done as a participant in the class. You see, my desire was that God would use each of the scriptures to impact my life. Having them in a separate journal enabled me, at quick glance, to see what God had done over the three-month journey!

Not only that, but through my journaling, I wanted to leave a legacy of what God has done throughout my life! The journal part of *Daughters of Sarah* is something I'll share with my children when they face struggles as adults. It documents the transformation performed by God and how I struggled to get to the other side of my sinful nature by His grace. I loved working *with* Him to become a woman of strength and dignity.

Getting Started

The Redeeming Work Journal is designed in a week-by-week format to be used during your daily Quiet Time with Him. You'll notice that it actually begins with Week 2. All that really means is that after you have attended

Session 1 of *Daughters of Sarah*, it's time to begin working through the journal.

I encourage you to open *The Redeeming Work Journal* daily. Read through the scriptures or just pick one to meditate upon. Again, there is no right or wrong way to do this, but **do begin in prayer,** asking God to direct your time with Him. Use these pages to pour out your heart to God, and take notes about what He reveals to you as you listen to Him. We frequently spend too much time listing our wants, needs, fears, etc., and very little time listening. I think you'll be pleasantly surprised as you learn to listen to His voice. This may show up in additional verses brought to mind, or in images that make little sense at the moment. Write them down, anyway, and ask Him for clarification.

Here's some ideas on how you might prayerfully consider using the journal:
- Write a letter to God, letting Him know how you are feeling, what you desire from the class, and anything else you might want to confess.
- Copy one of the scriptures, and write down how you want to apply it in your life.
- Put together a to-do list that you feel that God would have you pursue based on what He is teaching you through the course.
- Focus on one item from the class work as it relates to the class.
- Begin writing a prayer, using the words of scripture.
- Write the lyrics or chorus of a praise song or hymn. Ask the Lord why He has brought that to mind and record what you hear.

- Confess sin. Ask the Lord to show you how to repent and to repair any damages that may be attached to your sin.
- Describe how you are feeling. Some people find this helpful when trying to understand the *why* they are feeling the way that they are.

Again, whatever comes to mind is fine. Make it personal for you. Don't feel like you have to write on every line every week. The intent is for this to be **your soul work**.

Getting my feelings and desires down on paper allows me to leave the Master Potter to do His work in me. I hope you will have a similar experience.

I love the lyrics to an old hymn *Have Thine Own Way Lord*. May the words be the song of your heart as you go through these materials.

Have thine own way Lord! Have thine own way.
Thou art the potter, I am the clay.
Mold me and make me, after thy will.
While I am waiting, yielded and still.

May God richly bless you as you spend time with Him!

Debbie Hitchcock,
Operations Director of
Greater Impact Ministries

Week 2

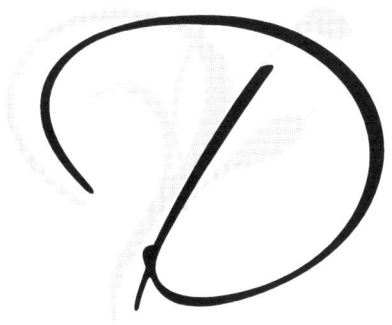

And this expectation will not disappoint us. For we know how dearly God loves us, because he has given us the Holy Spirit to fill our hearts with his love. When we were utterly helpless, Christ came at just the right time and died for us sinners. Now no one is likely to die for a good person, though someone might be willing to die for a person who is especially good. But God showed his great love for us by sending Christ to die for us while we were still sinners.
ROMANS 5:5-8

Love suffers long and is kind; love does not envy; love does not parade itself, is not puffed up; does not behave rudely, does not seek its own, is not provoked, thinks no evil; does not rejoice in iniquity, but rejoices in the truth; bears all things, believes all things, hopes all things, endures all things. Love never fails.
1 CORINTHIANS 13:4-8

God,

How is it that You love me this much?! My brain cannot wrap itself around the concept of such a love, that You would humble Yourself and become human, and then pay the price for all my sins. I think of my sins of yesterday, today and tomorrow, and how You have thrown them so far from Your sight – I just do not feel worthy of this gift of eternal life, knowing all the wrongs I have committed and will still.

But that is why it is called, "Grace," is it not? Your own son, the most perfect and holy creation You ever made, died for me. The love I experience for the humans I hold most dear is just a tiny fraction of the love You must have for us – to exchange my life for one of theirs… but to do what Christ did, to ransom his life, suffer the humiliation, the beating, the physical and emotional pain, to pay the eternity admittance fee for me before I even knew him… this great love is far beyond my human comprehension.

This incredible act of love moves me. Lord, fill me with the fullness of Your love and Your spirit. Help me love You with all my heart, with all my soul, and with all of my mind, and with all my strength. Give me longsuffering patience and kindness; keep me from envy, pride and rudeness; help me rejoice in truth and be worthy of You. Help me remember that You want the best for me and Your Word will guide me safely through life. Help me be obedient and not assume that I know better than You do, Lord. Help me know and keep Your commandments, and in this way, experience love for You and from You. I thank You for this opportunity and ask for Your blessings upon the days to come. Amen.

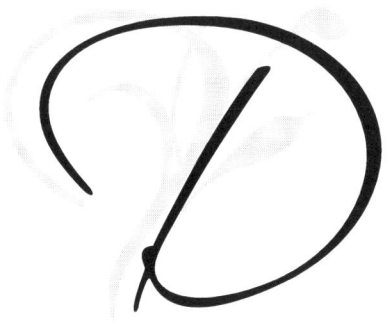# Week 3

Charm is deceptive and beauty is fleeting, but a woman who fears the Lord is to be praised.
PROVERBS 31:30

The beginning of wisdom is: Acquire wisdom; and with all your acquiring, get understanding.
PROVERBS 4:7

The fear of the Lord is the beginning of wisdom; a good understanding have all that do his commandments; his praise endures forever.
PSALM 111:10

The fear of the Lord is the beginning of wisdom, and knowledge of the Holy One is understanding.
PROVERBS 9:10

Oh Lord Most High, Creator of all things, Redeemer, Conqueror!

I praise You. I worship only You. Thank You for watching over me and everyone I hold dear. Thank You for my marriage. Thank You for this relationship which can grow me in Your ways and Your sight. Your ways are things I have trouble understanding; they are a mystery. But I will trust in Your sovereignty and believe in Your faithfulness. I want to know You more.

Father, help me be a wise woman. Help me be beautiful in Your sight. Create in me a new life, oh Lord, that I may be a new creation to better worship and serve Your purposes and not my own. Help me have an eternal perspective of marriage. Help me see it as yet but another opportunity to be obedient to Your Word. Enable me to spend time in Your Word and talk with You daily.

I desire wisdom, Father. I yearn to be pleasing in Your sight. I confess I have not been obedient as a wife and a woman of faith, and I have fallen short. Teach me, oh Lord. Show me where I can grow. Help me be a woman of strength and dignity, laughing at the days to come. Fan in me the flames of courage and enable me to obey Your Word. I praise Your name and thank You for the blessings in the days to come! May it all be for Your glory! Amen.

My dear brothers, take note of this: Everyone should be quick to listen, slow to speak and slow to become angry. ~**James 1:19**

The Lord is my rock and my fortress and my deliverer; My God, my strength, in whom I will trust; My shield and the horn of my salvation, my stronghold. ~**Psalm 18:2**

Do everything without complaining or arguing.
~Philippians 2:14

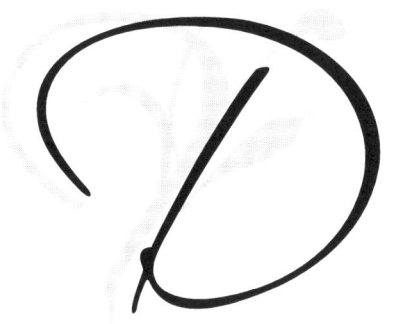# Week 4

For this reason I remind you to fan into flame the gift of God, which is in you through the laying on of my hands. For God did not give us a spirit of timidity, but a spirit of power, of love and of self-discipline.
2 TIMOTHY 1:6-7

The Lord has done great things for us, and we are filled with joy!
PSALM 126:3

Lord God Almighty!

Ruler of Everything, King of All Kings, I exalt thee! I praise thy holy name. Father, I thank You for my life, my marriage, my husband. I thank You that You have given me these things to draw me nearer to You. Father, help me become the woman You desire me to be. Help me be quick to listen, slow to speak, and slow to become angry when speaking with my husband. Help me do everything without complaint or argument. Keep my mouth pure and wholesome, and let me only speak what is helpful for building up my husband, even when I do not always feel that way. Help me overlook any insult from him; help me remember his good will toward me. Father, help me be wise with our money, and help me be thankful for what I have and not covet. Help me forgive him when he hurts me; let me not judge or condemn him, as I know I will be condemned and judged with the very measure I use for others.

Fill my thoughts during the day, Lord, with what is true, noble, right, pure, lovely, admirable, excellent and praiseworthy – help me think about such things and speak of them. Remove negativity from my thought life! Father, help me remember to ask my husband's advice and counsel, even when I think I can handle it or have dealt with the issue before. Father, keep me busy and in charge of my household duties, managing my children and their responsibilities. Help me not become idle. And when I open my mouth to speak, help me speak wisely and with a kind tongue. Help me do all these things, Lord, that Your teachings and Your Word be evidenced in my life. Amen.

Do not store up for yourselves treasures on earth, where moth and rust destroy, where thieves break in and steal. ~**Matthew 6:19**

Do not let any unwholesome talk come out of your mouths, but only what is helpful for building others up according to their needs, that it may benefit those who listen.
~Ephesians 4:29

A fool shows his annoyance at once, but a prudent man overlooks an insult.
~Proverbs 12:18

Week 5

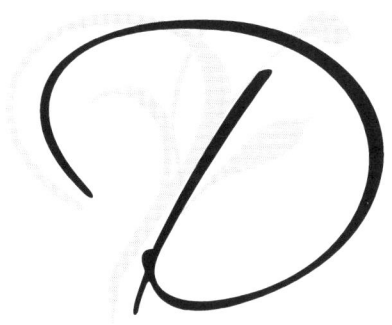

I can do all things through Christ who strengthens me.
PHILIPPIANS 4:13

The Lord has done great things for us and we are filled with joy!
PSALM 126:3

The Lord is my rock and my fortress and my deliverer; My God, my strength, in whom I will trust; My shield and the horn of my salvation, my stronghold.
PSALM 18:2

The Lord will open to you His good treasure, the heavens, to give the rain to your land in its season, and to bless all the work of your hand.
DEUTERONOMY 28:12A

Oh Lord, Most High God,

I praise You. I exalt You! You have done great things for me, and I am filled with joy when reflecting upon these blessings! You have gone out before me, Oh Lord. You have paved the way and cleared a path. I have sown in tears, and returned with sheaves of joy. It is to You I give the glory of the achievements in my life. You are my rock, my source of strength, and I cling to Your promises – I can do all things through Christ who strengthens me.

Father, I pray Your faithfulness be shown to me as I begin to live the life You have intended for me. You did not give me a spirit of timidity, but a spirit of power, of love, and of self-discipline. Your spirit is what I need to accomplish the work at hand. Father, I pray for Your spirit to be at work in my life, for my obedience, for Your purposes to be fulfilled. Help me see my marriage as another relationship that brings me closer to You; help me understand that You teach us and grow us through relationships with other people. I want to be useful to You, Lord. As You have used others to encourage me in my achievements, use me to encourage my husband as You so desire. It is the desire of my heart to be a wife that is pleasing to You, Father. How I long to hear, "Well done, my good and faithful servant!" upon my arrival at Your door. Create in me a new woman, a new wife, one that delights You and brings glory to Your name. Help me persevere in my own efforts and rely on Your strength. Guide me to wisdom, Father God.

Do not judge and you will not be judged. Do not condemn and you will not be condemned. Forgive and you will be forgiven. ~**Luke 6:37**

Finally brothers, whatever is true, whatever is noble, whatever is right, whatever is pure, whatever is lovely, whatever is admirable – if anything is excellent or praiseworthy – think about such things. ~**Philippians 4:8**

She opens her mouth in wisdom; and the teaching of kindness is on her tongue.
*~***Proverbs 31:26**

WEEK 6

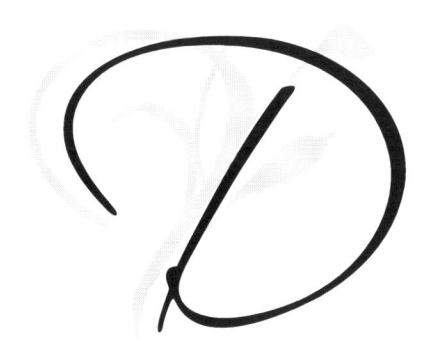

The Lord God said, "It is not good for the man to be alone, I will make a helper suitable for him."
GENESIS 2:18

Since he is the image and glory of God; but woman is the glory of man. For man is not from woman, but woman from man.
1 CORINTHIANS 11:7B-8

An excellent wife is the crown of her husband.
PROVERBS 12:4

Instead, it should be that of your inner self, the unfading beauty of a gentle and quiet spirit, which is of great worth in God's sight. For this is the way the holy women of the past who put their hope in God used to make themselves beautiful. They were submissive to their own husbands, like Sarah, who obeyed Abraham and called him her master. You are her daughters if you do what is right and do not give way to fear.
1 PETER 3:4-6

Father,

I praise You for making my husband so different from me. Because of these differences, I know he is not trying to hurt me; he just communicates and thinks differently than I do. Father, I praise You that You made this man in Your image, and I see that when I respect him, I am respecting You. I understand that I can demonstrate my understanding of Your worthiness by how I communicate about men in general. Father, let my words be praiseworthy and glorifying to You.

I regret all the times I demeaned men with my words because in effect, I was demeaning You, as they are created in Your perfect image. Forgive me for the times I made fun of men or treated my husband like a child. You created me to be a helper for my man. I see now that I am a reflection of Your glory for my husband. Help me live up to this high position. Help me respond to all the men in my life in ways that communicate respect and appropriate affirmation of their manhood.

Help me model this for my children. Help me understand what submission means in my life, Father. I know that esteeming my husband and affirming his position as head of our home helps protect him from getting this need met elsewhere. Help me be the kind of wife that my husband is proud to call his. I pray to emulate the Proverbs 31 woman, whose husband has full confidence in her. Help me see myself as beautiful in Your sight. Guide me into the behaviors that make me lovely to You and my husband. I yearn for my man to say of me, "many women do noble things, but You surpass them all." Help me be a crown for my husband, Lord; help me glorify You and him in this way. Amen.

She watches over the affairs of her household and does not eat the bread of idleness.
~**Proverbs** *31:27*

Do not judge and you will not be judged. Do not condemn and you will not be condemned. Forgive and you will be forgiven. ~**Luke 6:37**

Do not store up for yourselves treasures on earth, where moth and rust destroy, where thieves break in and steal. **~Matthew 6:19**

Week 7

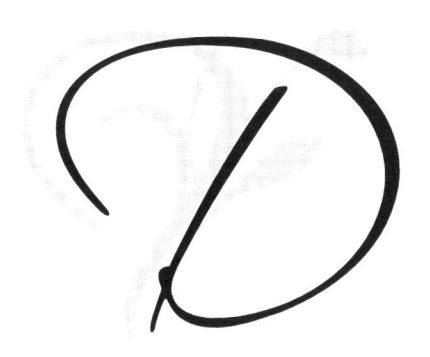

...so that they may encourage the young women to love their husbands, to love their children, to be sensible, pure, workers at home, kind, being subject to their own husbands, so that the Word of God will not be dishonored.
TITUS 2:4-5

An excellent wife is the crown of her husband, but she who causes shame is like rottenness in his bones.
PROVERBS 12:4

...and the wife see that she reverence her husband.
EPHESIANS 5:33

Reckless words pierce like a sword, but the tongue of the wise brings healing.
PROVERBS 12:18

Heavenly Father,

I praise Your Holy Name! None but You know true righteousness! That You would even bid me come into Your presence is beyond all comprehension. Father, help me be strong in You and Your mighty power. Help me be clothed in Your strength, Your dignity, so that when evil comes, I can stand my ground firmly against it, with the belt of truth buckled around my waist.

Clothe me with the breastplate of righteousness in place, and with my feet fitted with the readiness that comes from the gospel of peace. Hand me Your shield of faith, with which the arrows of evil are extinguished. Place the helmet of salvation upon my head, and the sword of the Spirit, which is the Word of God, in my hands. Help me willingly place myself subject to my husband, that he might be my protection and my knight.

Father, help me understand my husband's need to be his friend. Show me ways to communicate friendship to him. Help me see this communicates my love to him in a way that is meaningful and important to him. Help me have the self-control and discipline and respectful communication it will take. Show me how to be his best friend, a person he wants to be with most of all. Help me be the wife You desire me to be, Lord. Amen.

She opens her mouth in wisdom; and the teaching of kindness is on her tongue.
~Proverbs 31:26

Finally brothers, whatever is true, whatever is noble, whatever is right, whatever is pure, whatever is lovely, whatever is admirable – if anything is excellent or praiseworthy – think about such things. ~**Philippians 4:8**

Carry each other's burdens, and in this way you will fulfill the law of Christ. ~**Galatians 6:2**

WEEK 8

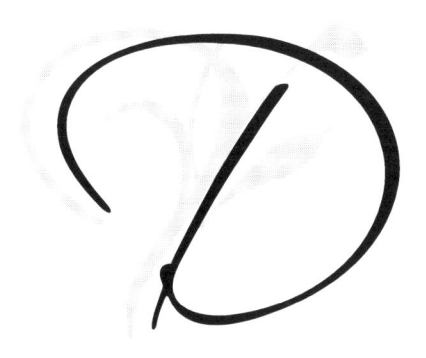

And have you entirely forgotten the encouraging words God spoke to you, his children? He said, "My child, don't ignore it when the Lord disciplines you, and don't be discouraged when he corrects you. For the Lord disciplines those he loves, and he punishes those he accepts as his children." As you endure this divine discipline, remember that God is treating you as his own children.
HEBREWS 12:5-6

No discipline is enjoyable while it is happening – it is painful! But afterward there will be a quiet harvest of right living for those who are trained in this way. So take a new grip with your tired hands and stand firm on your shaky legs. Mark out a straight path for your feet. Then those who follow you, though they are weak and lame, will not stumble and fall but will become strong.
HEBREWS 12:11-13

In the same way, you wives must accept the authority of your husbands, even those who refuse to accept the Good News. Your godly lives will speak to them better than any words. They will be won over by watching your pure, godly behavior. Don't be concerned about the outward beauty that depends on fancy hairstyles, expensive jewelry, or beautiful clothes. You should be known for the beauty that comes from within, the unfading beauty of a gentle and quiet spirit, which is so precious to God. That is the way the holy women of old made themselves beautiful. They trusted God and accepted the authority of their husbands. For instance, Sarah obeyed her husband, Abraham, when she called him her master. You are her daughters when you do what is right without fear of what your husbands might do.
1 PETER 3:1-6

Father,

I praise Your name for the changes You are making in me — I'm becoming new in You again and again; You make all things new, and in me a good and mighty work is being done to bring glory to Your name. Thank You! It's not easy to make changes, Lord. It's hard to have the unfruitful parts of myself pruned so I can bear more fruit. It even hurts. I thank You that You love me enough to work in me, Lord. I pray that what I am becoming be a blessing to the future generations in my family and other young people in my circle of influence because of the wife I am becoming. I pray for endurance in this race, Lord. Strip off every weight that slows me down, especially the sin that so easily hinders my progress. Let me run with endurance this race You've set before me, Father. Keep my eyes on Jesus, on whom my faith depends from start to finish. Thank You, Father!

BE AWARE...BE WISE...

Father in Heaven,

I know Your Word spends more time addressing "fear" than sin – and I am well aware that whatever I pay attention to grows. The enemy of my soul is on the prowl, looking for someone to devour! The women who have walked before me through Daughters of Sarah have learned this. Help me learn from their experience, Lord. Help me focus on what You are accomplishing in my life. Help me always refer to how I was before I took the class, and reveal Your blessings again to me. Forbid the enemy from blinding me to my growth and the great blessings that come from obedience to You – keep me from being tricked by him, and show me Your way.

I might be tempted...to give way to fear...to compare myself to someone else in class...to see my husband in a negative light because he did not respond the way I thought he should...to forget what You have done and are doing...or to minimize Your work in my life – I ask that as I come to the sessions where I am to bring glory to Your name by talking about these things that You open my eyes and help me claim victory!

Make me strong in You, Lord, and in Your mighty power! Place on me the full armor of You, so I can take my stand against the enemy's schemes. Help me remember that my struggle is not against flesh and blood, but against the rulers, against the authorities, against the powers of this dark world and against the spiritual forces of evil in the heavenly realms.

With Your help, I can stand firm, with the belt of truth buckled around my waist, with the breastplate of righteousness in place, and with my feet fitted with the readiness that comes from the gospel of peace. In addition to all this, help me take up the shield of faith, with which I can extinguish all the flaming arrows of the evil one. I take the helmet of salvation and the sword of the Spirit, which is the Word of God. And help me pray in the Spirit on all occasions, with all kinds of prayers and requests, keep me alert and praying for all the saints, and especially my husband and family. Whatever I pay attention to grows – help me focus on YOU!

Protect me from thoughts of failure, defeat and dismay. Keep from me the temptation to compare myself to the other women, or to judge my "successes" in a worldy sense – remind me that it's not my husband's behavior I am seeking to change, but rather my own heart and walk with You that needs growth. Protect me from any seeds of jealousy the enemy might try to sow in me, and show me what is good, noble, right, pure, lovely, admirable, excellent and praiseworthy in all situations! Keep my eyes turned upon Jesus!

Thank You, for Jesus, for the war being won, thank You for Your protection! May I glorify You with my life, may You make me brave for Your glory, may my life's song sing to You and make You smile…in Christ Jesus, Amen.

If they want to inquire about something, they should ask their own husbands at home.
~1 Corinthians 14:35

Do not let any unwholesome talk come out of your mouths, but only what is helpful for building others up according to their needs, that it may benefit those who listen.
~Ephesians 4:29

Carry each other's burdens, and in this way you will fulfill the law of Christ. ~**Galatians 6:2**

Week 9

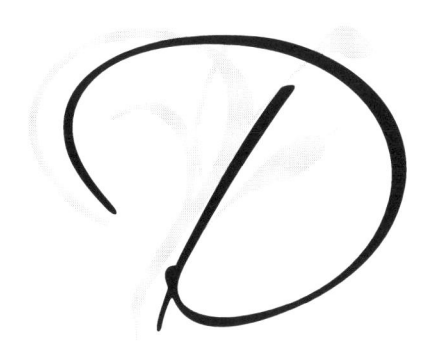

The wise woman builds her house, but the foolish tears it down with her own hands.
PROVERBS 14:1

But because of your stubbornness and your unrepentant heart, you are storing up wrath against yourself for the day of God's wrath, when his righteous judgment will be revealed.
ROMANS 2:5

But in all these things, we overwhelmingly conquer through Him who loved us. For I am convinced that neither death, nor life, nor angels, nor principalities, nor things present, nor things to come, nor powers, nor height, nor depth, nor any other created thing, will be able to separate us from the love of God, which is in Christ Jesus, our Lord.
ROMANS 8:37-39

Creator of All Things, Omniscient Everlasting Lord!

I praise You and lift Your name on high! Your eternal perspective is so perfect; thank You for beginning this work in me! I long for the days in Your kingdom, where praises will never cease. Father, whatever I do, help me do it heartily, as for You, rather than for others – knowing that from You I will receive my reward. Remind me, Lord, that it is Christ Jesus I serve, when I am subject to my husband. Help me build my house, one that glorifies You. Bind my tongue. Tame it such that I do not tear down all that I am creating with Your help. Forgive me for the unkind and disrespectful words I have spoken to my husband or other men, Father. Forgive my stubborn attitude and unwillingness to let him lead.

Show me my temptation to step in front of him, to usurp his authority. Help me be subject to my husband and teach me what that means. Remind me that my husband is not someone else's husband, so what works in their marriage may be different in ours. Show me, Lord, what this means and what blessings will come of it. I do not understand this mystery. Give me a teachable spirit, Lord, and show me the blessings of obedience! It is my heart's desire to be like Jesus. You encourage, comfort, and urge me to live a life worthy of Your precious Son. Father, Let the word of Christ dwell in me richly as I teach and encourage other women through my experiences in this class. Whatever I do, Lord, whether in word or deed, let me do it all in the name of Lord Jesus, giving thanks to You, Father, through Him. Thank You that nothing separates me from Your love, O Lord!

BE AWARE…BE WISE…

Father in Heaven,

Help me judge wisely what I should share with the women this week! Help me stay focused on my obedience, and the intrinsic reward therein …and NOT on the "world's view" of "success." The enemy of my soul would have me tattoo a big "loser" sign on my forehead and judge my efforts as unworthy of You - The women who have walked before me through Daughters of Sarah have experienced this same trick. Help me learn from their experience, Lord. Help me focus on what You are accomplishing in my life. Help me always remember that my heart is seen by You and You are pleased when I am obedient, regardless of the measure of the "success." Forbid the enemy from blinding me.

I might be tempted…to give way to fear…to compare myself to someone else in class…to see my husband in a negative light because he did not respond the way I thought he should…to forget what You have done and are doing…to feel bad because my whole goal wasn't realized…or to minimize Your work in my life – I ask that as I come to the sessions where I am to bring glory to Your name by talking about these things that You open my eyes and help me claim victory!

Make me strong in You, Lord, and in Your mighty power! Place on me the full armor of You, so I can take my stand against the enemy's schemes. Help me remember that my struggle is not against flesh and blood, but against the rulers, against the authorities, against the powers of this dark world and against the spiritual forces of evil in the heavenly realms.

With Your help, I can stand firm, with the belt of truth buckled around my waist, with the breastplate of righteousness in place, and with my feet fitted with the readiness that comes from the gospel of peace. In addition to all this, help me take up the shield of faith, with which I can extinguish all the flaming arrows of the evil one. I take the helmet of salvation and the sword of the Spirit, which is the Word of God. And help me pray in the Spirit on all occasions, with all kinds of prayers and requests, keep me alert and praying for all the saints, and especially my husband and family. Whatever I pay attention to grows — help me focus on YOU!

Father, I offer my efforts as a love sacrifice to You, worthy of Your name. I am seeking to change, to grow into the woman of obedience that is beautiful to Your eyes. Protect me from any seeds of jealousy the enemy might try to sow in me, and show me what is good, noble, right, pure, lovely, admirable, excellent and praiseworthy in all situations! Keep my eyes turned upon Jesus!

Thank You, for Jesus, for the war being won, thank You for Your protection! May I glorify You with my life, may You make me brave for Your glory, may my life's song sing to You and make You smile…in Christ Jesus, Amen.

*Keep your lives free from the love of money and be content with what you have, because God has said, "Never will I leave you; never will I forsake you." ~**Hebrews 13:5***

Pleasant words are a honeycomb, sweet to the soul and healing to the bones. ~**Proverbs 16:24**

She brings him good, not harm, all the days of her life. ~*Proverbs 31:12*

Week 10

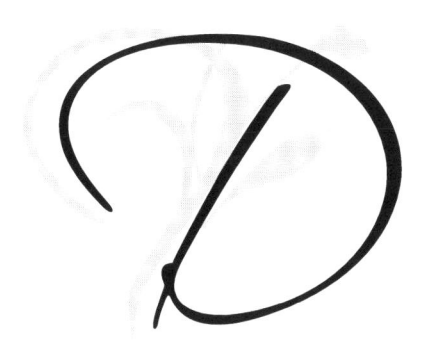

An excellent wife is the crown of her husband, but she who causes shame is like rottenness in his bones.
PROVERBS 12:4

The wife does not have authority over her own body, but the husband does. And likewise, the husband does not have authority over his own body, but the wife does. Do not deprive one another except with consent for a time, that You may give Yourselves to fasting and prayer; and come together again so that Satan does not tempt You because of Your lack of self-control.
1 CORINTHIANS 7:4-5

Wives, be subject to your own husbands, as to the Lord. For the husband is the head of the wife, as Christ also is the head of the church, He Himself being the Savior of the body. But as the church is subject to Christ, so also the wives ought to be to their husbands in everything.
EPHESIANS 5:22-24

Heavenly Father, Merciful God!

I am in awe of You! Father, I pray to be pleasing in Your sight! Help me understand what it means to affirm and encourage my man, Father. Make me responsive every time he is interested in sex, Lord. Help me initiate intimacy more often, Lord, and if he isn't interested in me, help me respect that and not take it personally.

Help us work through any issues we have with sex, Lord, such that I am capable of affirming him as a man in this way. Father, I invite You into our bedroom and ask that You bless our physical union. May we glorify You in our being together sexually. Father, I ask that You teach me about submission. Help me understand what I gain, what my family gains, by my understanding of this concept.

Help me see the blessings that You bestow upon those of us who are obedient in this way. It isn't easy, Lord. Our culture makes "submission" a bad word, and I confess I neither fully understand it, nor do I always act in this way. Help me figure out how to be my husband's friend, helper and partner in this life without becoming a doormat or domineering woman. Where is the balance in my marriage, Lord? Please show me and help me communicate to my husband about these things. Help me glorify You by my actions as a wife, Lord. Help me hear the words of the women that do understand, Father. May my obedience to this command glorify You – help me willingly lay down my stubborn spirit and exchange it for a gentle and quiet one that brings honor to Your Word. Amen.

John 14

15 "If you love me, you will obey what I command. **16** And I will ask the Father, and he will give you another Counselor to be with you forever-- **17** the Spirit of truth. The world cannot accept him, because it neither sees him nor knows him. But you know him, for he lives with you and will be in you.

18 I will not leave you as orphans; I will come to you. **19** Before long, the world will not see me anymore, but you will see me. Because I live, you also will live. **20** On that day you will realize that I am in my Father, and you are in me, and I am in you. **21** Whoever has my commands and obeys them, he is the one who loves me. He who loves me will be loved by my Father, and I too will love him and show myself to him." **22** Then Judas (not Judas Iscariot) said, "But, Lord, why do you intend to show yourself to us and not to the world?" **23** Jesus replied, "If anyone loves me, he will obey my teaching. My Father will love him, and we will come to him and make our home with him. **24** He who does not love me will not obey my teaching. These words you hear are not my own; they belong to the Father who sent me.

25 "All this I have spoken while still with you. **26** But the Counselor, the Holy Spirit, whom the Father will send in my name, will teach you all things and will remind you of everything I have said to you.
27 Peace I leave with you; my peace I give you. I do not give to you as the world gives. Do not let your hearts be troubled and do not be afraid.

28 "You heard me say, 'I am going away and I am coming back to you.' If you loved me, you would be glad that I am going to the Father, for the Father is greater than I. **29** I have told you now before it happens, so that when it does happen you will believe. **30** I will not speak with you much longer, for the prince of this world is coming. He has no hold on me, **31** but the world must learn that I love the Father and that I do exactly what my Father has commanded me. "Come now; let us leave.

John 15

1 "I am the true vine, and my Father is the gardener. *2* He cuts off every branch in me that bears no fruit, while every branch that does bear fruit he prunes so that it will be even more fruitful. *3* You are already clean because of the word I have spoken to you. *4* Remain in me, and I will remain in you. No branch can bear fruit by itself; it must remain in the vine. Neither can you bear fruit unless you remain in me. *5* "I am the vine; you are the branches. If a man remains in me and I in him, he will bear much fruit; apart from me you can do nothing. *6* If anyone does not remain in me, he is like a branch that is thrown away and withers; such branches are picked up, thrown into the fire and burned. *7* If you remain in me and my words remain in you, ask whatever you wish, and it will be given you. *8* This is to my Father's glory, that you bear much fruit, showing yourselves to be my disciples.

9 "As the Father has loved me, so have I loved you. Now remain in my love. *10* If you obey my commands, you will remain in my love, just as I have obeyed my Father's commands and remain in his love. *11* I have told you this so that my joy may be in you and that your joy may be complete.

12 My command is this: Love each other as I have loved you.
13 Greater love has no one than this, that he lay down his life for his friends. *14* You are my friends if you do what I command. *15* I no longer call you servants, because a servant does not know his master's business. Instead, I have called you friends, for everything that I learned from my Father I have made known to you. *16* You did not choose me, but I chose you and appointed you to go and bear fruit--fruit that will last. Then the Father will give you whatever you ask in my name. *17* This is my command: Love each other.

Questions:

1. What are the common themes in the passages in John 14 and John 15?

　_____
　_____
　_____
　_____
　_____
　_____
　_____
　_____
　_____
　_____
　_____

2. What are the correlations between these passages and the experience you have had in Daughters of Sarah®?

　_____
　_____
　_____
　_____
　_____
　_____
　_____
　_____
　_____
　_____

3. What is the difference between yielding to change at His hand and constant striving for obedience?

_____
_____
_____
_____
_____
_____
_____
_____
_____
_____

4. Why does this matter?

_____
_____
_____
_____
_____
_____
_____
_____
_____
_____

For God is not a God of disorder but of peace…But everything should be done in a fitting and orderly way.
~1 Corinthians 14:33, 40

Do nothing from selfishness or empty conceit, but with humility of mind regard one another as more important than yourselves; do not merely look out for your own personal interests, but also for the interests of others.
~*Philippians 2:3-4*

And we know that all things work together for good for those who love God, and are called according to his purpose.
~Romans 8:28

Week 11

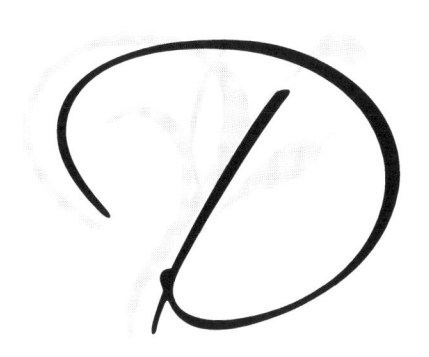

Therefore gird up the loins of your mind, be sober, and rest your hope fully upon the grace that is to be brought to you at the revelation of Jesus Christ; as obedient children, not conforming yourselves to the former lusts, as in your ignorance; but as He who called you is holy, you also be holy in all your conduct, because it is written, "Be holy for I am holy."
1 PETER 1:13-16

Since you have purified your souls in obeying the truth through the Spirit in sincere love of the brethren, love one another fervently with a pure heart, having been born again, not of corruptible seed but incorruptible, through the Word of God which lives and abides forever.
1 PETER 1:22-23

For to this you were called, because Christ also suffered for us, leaving us an example, that you should follow His steps: "Who committed no sin, nor was deceit found in His mouth"; who, when He was reviled, did not revile in return; when He suffered, He did not threaten, but committed Himself to Him who judges righteously;
1 PETER 2:21-23

Wives, likewise, be submissive to your own husbands, that even if some do not obey the word, they without a word, will be won by the conduct of their wives.
1 PETER 3:1

Wonderful Savior, Beautiful One, Holiest of Holies,

You are my Stronghold! I am thinking of Michal, who was barren as a result of her contempt for David's unashamed dancing in worship of You, Father. I am sorry for the times I have spoken to my own husband in a contemptuous way. Forgive me! I have stepped out in front of him, Lord, as well. Not so much unlike Jezebel and Eve, I have taken matters into my own hands because I have not trusted him. I see it is really You I have not trusted. Redeemer, I understand why the pruning shears have to have such sharp edges!

Help me rest my hope fully in You, Father. Purify my soul in obedience to Your Word. Help me respond in love, even when my husband's words revile me. I love him, Lord, and his words hurt me sometimes. I see that following in the footsteps of Christ is not free from pain, but I so desire to be pleasing in Your sight, Lord. Continue this work in me, Lord, that I might truly respond in love as Christ. Make me beautiful in Your sight.

I am eager for the peace and joy that flow out of my obedience to Your Word! I know from this refining, this pruning, I will emerge more useful to You, more of a blessing to others, an instrument of Your everlasting love. "Likewise" applies to me, too, Lord. Show me the way. Amen.

BE AWARE… BE WISE…

Father in Heaven,

Your perfect Word spends more time addressing "fear" than sin – and I am well aware that whatever I pay attention to grows. The enemy of my soul is on the prowl, looking for someone to devour! The women who have walked before me through Daughters of Sarah have learned this. Help me learn from their experience, Lord. Help me focus on what You are accomplishing in my life. Help me always refer to how I was before I took the class, and reveal Your blessings again to me. Forbid the enemy from blinding me to my growth and the great blessings that come from obedience to You – keep me from being tricked by him, and show me Your way.

I might be tempted…to give way to fear…to compare myself to someone else in class…to see my husband in a negative light because he did not respond the way I thought he should…to forget what You have done and are doing…or to minimize Your work in my life – I ask that as I come to the sessions where I am to bring glory to Your name by talking about these things that You open my eyes and help me claim victory!

Make me strong in You, Lord, and in Your mighty power! Place on me the full armor of You, so I can take my stand against the enemy's schemes. Help me remember that my struggle is not against flesh and blood, but against the rulers, against the authorities, against the powers of this dark world and against the spiritual forces of evil in the heavenly realms.

With Your help, I can stand firm, with the belt of truth buckled around my waist, with the breastplate of righteousness in place, and with my feet fitted with the readiness that comes from the gospel of peace. In addition to all this, help me take up the shield of faith, with which I can extinguish all the flaming arrows of the evil one. I take the helmet of salvation and the sword of the Spirit, which is the Word of God. And help me pray in the Spirit on all occasions, with all kinds of prayers and requests, keep me alert and praying for all the saints, and especially my husband and family. Whatever I pay attention to grows – help me focus on YOU!

Protect me from thoughts of failure, defeat and dismay. Keep from me the temptation to compare myself to the other women, or to judge my "successes" in a worldy sense – remind me that it's not my husband's behavior I am seeking to change, but rather my own heart and walk with You that needs growth. Protect me from any seeds of jealousy the enemy might try to sow in me, and show me what is good, noble, right, pure, lovely, admirable, excellent and praiseworthy in all situations! Keep my eyes turned upon Jesus!

Thank You, for Jesus, for the war being won, thank You for Your protection! May I glorify You with my life, may You make me brave for Your glory, may my life's song sing to You and make You smile…in Christ Jesus, Amen.

And the wife must respect her husband.
~Ephesians 5:33b

For God is not a God of disorder but of peace…But everything should be done in a fitting and orderly way.
~1 Corinthians 14:33, 40

Whatever you do, do your work heartily, as for the Lord, rather than for men, knowing that from the Lord you will receive the reward of the inheritance. It is Christ whom you serve.
~Colossians 3:23-34

Week 12

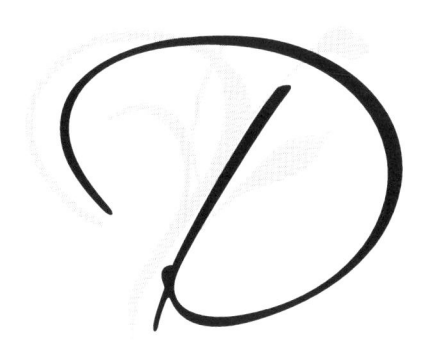

Therefore if you are presenting your offering at the altar, and there remember that your brother has something against you, leave your offering there before the altar and go; first be reconciled to your brother, and then come and present your offering.
MATTHEW 5:23

I plead with Euodia and I plead with Syntyche to agree with each other in the Lord.
PHILIPPIANS 4:2

Pride goes before destruction, and a haughty spirit before stumbling.
PROVERBS 16:18

If you, O Lord, kept a record of sins, O Lord, who could stand? But with you there is forgiveness; therefore you are feared.
PSALM 130:3, 4

Make every effort to live in peace with all men and to be holy; without holiness no one will see the Lord.
HEBREWS 12:14

He who guards his lips guards his life, but he who speaks rashly will come to ruin.
PROVERBS 13:3

If anyone considers himself religious and yet does not keep a tight rein on his tongue, he deceives himself and his religion is worthless.
JAMES 1:26

He who answers before listening, that is his folly and his shame.
PROVERBS 18:13

A gentle answer turns away wrath, but a harsh word stirs up anger.
PROVERBS 15:1

In your anger do not sin; do not let the sun go down while you are still angry.
EPHESIANS 4:26

Starting a quarrel is like breaching a dam; so drop the matter before a dispute breaks out.
PROVERBS 17:14

It is to a man's honor to avoid strife, but every fool is quick to quarrel.
PROVERBS 20:3

Do not let any unwholesome talk come out of your mouths, but only what is helpful for building others up according to their needs, that it may benefit those who listen.
EPHESIANS 4:29

A gossip betrays a confidence; so avoid a man who talks too much.
PROVERBS 20:19

Do you see a man who speaks in haste? There is more hope for a fool than for him.
PROVERBS 29:20

When words are many, sin is not absent, but he who holds his tongue is wise.
PROVERBS 10: 19

Therefore, as God's chosen people, holy and dearly loved, clothe yourselves with compassion, kindness, humility, gentleness and patience. Bear with each other and forgive whatever grievances you may have against one another. Forgive as the Lord forgave you. And over all these virtues put on love, which binds them all together in perfect unity.
COLOSSIANS 3:12-14

See that no one repays another with evil for evil, but always seek after that which is good for one another and for all people.
1 THESSALONIANS 5:13

Love is patient, love is kind. It does not envy, it does not boast, it is not proud. It is not rude, it is not self-seeking, it is not easily angered, it keeps no record of wrongs. Love does not delight in evil but rejoices with the truth. It always protects, always trusts, always hopes, always perseveres. Love never fails.
1 CORINTHIANS 13:4-8A

A wise man's heart guides his mouth, and his lips promote instruction. Pleasant words are a honeycomb, sweet to the soul and healing to the bones.
PROVERBS 16:23-24

A man of knowledge uses words with restraint, and a man of understanding is even-tempered.
PROVERBS 17:27

Even a fool is thought wise if he keeps silent, and discerning if he holds his tongue.
PROVERBS 17:28

Heavenly Father,

It is no mistake Your son is the Prince of Peace! It is my heart's desire that my relationship with my husband be pleasing to You, and the way I deal with differences of opinion or disagreements make You smile. Help me keep my stubborn pride in check, Lord. Let me be flexible enough to listen and bend! I pray to abandon the list of hurts and grievances I have toward my husband. Help my forgiveness be as true and permanent as Yours.

Help me to keep a tight rein on my tongue, let me not speak in anger, regardless of how I am spoken to — help me model Christ in this way! Father, I know that Satan is the father of lies and that he would have me believe my husband's intentions are mean-spirited. You remind me that my husband is a good-willed man, so help me not to perpetuate the lie; help me see the truth. Lord, when I am angry at my husband, keep me from sinning. Help me keep my mouth shut and speak gently to him. Instead of demanding my "rights" or "needs" be met, grant me Your supernatural patience to wait for something to thank him and give him praise for. Remind me that whatever I pay attention to will grow. Let me often give my husband and others the "benefit of the doubt," and let all talk coming out of my mouth be helpful for building up, rather than tearing down. Often my assumptions are wrong, Lord. Keep me silent until I know the truth.

Clothe me with compassion, kindness, humility, gentleness and patience. Help me bear with my husband and others. Help me forgive when I am hurt. Bind all these virtues with love in perfect unity within me, Father. Help me resist the temptation to "show him how it feels" and repay evil for evil. Help me keep from sinning in this regard! I know he is not my enemy and my battle is not with flesh and blood. Keep me from giving into this trick. Teach me to be patient and kind. Keep me from envy, boasting and pride. Help me be polite and selfless, long-suffering and not easily angered, keeping no record of wrongs! Help me rejoice in Your truth.

Help me protect my relationship with my husband, hope for the best, and persevere through our trials. Give me endurance for holiness… becoming like Christ through this context of marriage is not easy! But Your perfect love never fails, Father! Let my words to my husband be sweet as honey to his soul and healing to his bones. Teach me, mold me, and make me, O Potter. I am but "unfashioned" clay in Your expert hands. Create in me a beauty that pleases You! Amen.

To sum up, all of you be harmonious, sympathetic, brotherly, kind-hearted, and humble in spirit, not returning evil for evil or insult for insult, but giving a blessing instead; for you were called for the very purpose that you might inherit a blessing. ~*1 Peter 3:8, 9*

They may be won without a word by the behavior of their wives, as they observe your chaste and respectful behavior. ~*1 Peter 3:16, 2*

I appeal to you, brothers, in the name of our Lord Jesus Christ, that all of you agree with one another so that there may be no divisions among you and that you may be perfectly united in mind and thought.
~1 Corinthians 1:10

Week 13

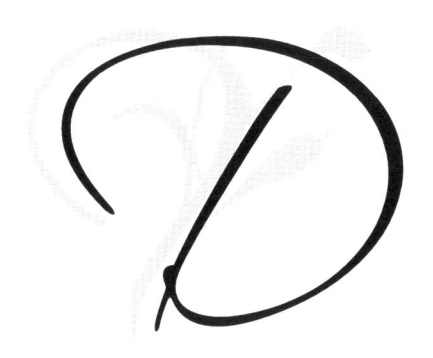

You've had a taste of God. Now, like infants at the breast, drink deep of God's pure kindness. Then you'll grow up mature and whole in God.
1 PETER 2:1-3

You also, as living stones, are being built up a spiritual house, a holy priesthood, to offer up spiritual sacrifices acceptable to God through Jesus Christ.
1 PETER 2:5

This is the kind of life you've been invited into, the kind of life Christ lived. He suffered everything that came his way so you would know that it could be done, and also know how to do it, step-by-step.
PETER 2:21

The Lord has done great things for us, and we are filled with Joy!
PSALM 126:3

Those who sow in tears shall reap in joy. He who continually goes forth weeping, bearing seed for sowing, shall doubtless come again with rejoicing, bringing his sheaves with him.
PSALM 126:5-6

Wonderful Savior, Beautiful One, Redeemer, Name Above All Names!

You alone are worthy of praise! That You died for me, that You bled for me, that You bore my sin as the ultimate sacrifice... I am at a loss to understand this kind of love, Lord! I praise You, Father, for being the kind of God that makes a way for his children to not just survive, but to succeed and emerge from trials and pain victorious! I see that You are refining me into someone useful for Your purposes.

I see now that whenever I endure difficulty, it is tremendously important that I do so with grace, strength and dignity. When Your glory is revealed, I know I will be filled with exceeding joy! Father, the results of my obedience are not always readily obvious. Sometimes it takes a while for me to see Your purpose, but I trust You, Father, and I know that all things work together for good for those that love You and are called according to Your purpose.

Thank You, Father, for choosing me for Your child. What a privilege it is to be in Your family! Amen.

BE AWARE… BE WISE…

Father in Heaven,

Help me choose wisely what I should share with the women this week! I want to be a blessing to them, and motivate them to follow Your commands. Help me stay focused on my obedience, and the intrinsic reward that in itself is…NOT on the "world's view" of "success" or my husband's behavior! The enemy of my soul would have me judge my efforts as unworthy of You - The women who have walked before me through Daughters of Sarah have experienced this same trick. Help me learn from their experience, Lord. Help me focus on what You are accomplishing in my life. Help me always remember that my heart is seen by You and You are pleased when I am obedient, regardless of the measure of the "results". My efforts are for Your glory.

I might be tempted…to give way to fear…to compare myself to someone else in class…to see my husband in a negative light because he did not respond the way I thought he should…to forget what You have done and are doing…to feel bad because my whole goal wasn't realized…or to minimize Your work in my life — I ask that as I come to the sessions where I can bring glory to Your name by talking about these things, that You open my eyes and help me claim victory! Remind me to resist temptation!

Make me strong in You, Lord, and in Your mighty power! Place on me the full armor of You, so I can take my stand against the enemy's schemes. Help me remember that my struggle is not against flesh and blood, but against the rulers, against the authorities, against the powers of this dark world and against the spiritual forces of evil in the heavenly realms. With Your help, I can stand firm, with the belt of truth buckled around my waist, with the breastplate of righteousness in place, and with my feet fitted with the readiness that comes from the gospel of peace. In addition to all this, help me take up the shield of faith, with which I can extinguish all the flaming arrows of the evil one. I take the helmet of salvation and the sword of the Spirit, which is the Word of God. Help me pray in the Spirit on all occasions, with all kinds of prayers and requests, keep me alert and praying for all the saints, and especially for my husband and family. Whatever I pay attention to grows – help me focus on YOU!

Father, I offer my efforts as a love sacrifice to You, worthy of Your name. I am seeking to change, to grow into the woman of obedience that is beautiful in Your eyes. Protect me from any seeds of jealousy the enemy might try to sow in me, and show me what is good, noble, right, pure, lovely, admirable, excellent and praiseworthy in all situations! Keep my eyes turned upon Jesus!

Thank You, for Jesus, for the war being won, thank You for Your protection! May I glorify You with my life, may You make me brave for Your glory, may my life's song sing to You and make You smile…in Christ Jesus, Amen.

But encourage one another daily, as long as it is called Today, so that none of you may be hardened by sin's deceitfulness.
~Hebrews 3:13

Like a gold ring in a pig's snout is a beautiful woman who shows no discretion.
~Proverbs 11:22

And let us consider how we may spur one another on toward love and good deeds.
~Hebrews 10:24

Week 14

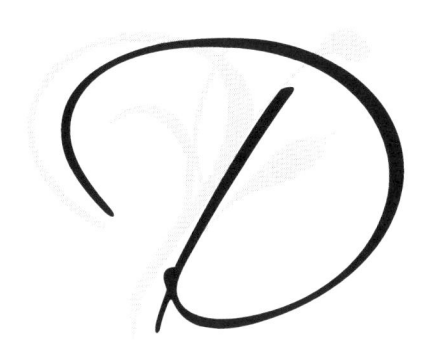

The Lord has done great things for us and we are filled with Joy!
PSALM 126:3

Always be joyful. Keep on praying. No matter what happens, always be thankful, for this is God's will for you who belong to Christ Jesus.
1 THESSALONIANS 5:16-18

…The earnest prayer of a righteous person has great power and wonderful results.
JAMES 5:16

…acknowledge the God of your father, and serve him with wholehearted devotion and with a willing mind, for the Lord searches every heart and understands every motive behind the thoughts.
1 CHRONICLES 28:9A

…let your good deeds shine out for all to see, so that everyone will praise your heavenly Father.
MATTHEW 5:16

And I am sure that God, who began the good work within you, will continue His work until it is finally finished on that day when Christ Jesus comes back again.
PHILIPPIANS 1:6

For this very reason, make every effort to add to your faith goodness…knowledge…self-control…perseverance…godliness…brotherly kindness…love. For if you possess these qualities in increasing measure, they will keep you from being ineffective and unproductive in your knowledge of our Lord Jesus Christ.
2 PETER 1:5-8

Heavenly Father,

I praise Your awesome Name! It is with incredible thanksgiving that I lift Your name on high – and with great joy I thank You for this teaching! Father, bless this new beginning; help me to walk in obedience and to become more like Jesus. Keep my focus on You as I walk through the remaining days of my marriage. I know from scripture that You hate divorce – and now I understand that my marriage is the context in which I become holy. Thank You for loving me enough to give me this opportunity at refinement.

Thank You for giving me the blueprint of obedience through Your Word. Hold my hand the rest of the way, Father, until I see You in heaven. Be with me always, and never let me turn from you. Draw me nearer, hold me close, and mold me into the daughter You desire me to be! Amen.

BE AWARE... BE WISE...

Father in Heaven,

How I long to bring glory to Your name this special night – show me what I should speak about, and help me communicate it well. Remind me of the changes You have knit into the fiber of my soul – help me remember how far I have come since the information meeting! Help me focus on what You are accomplishing in my life. Help me always refer to how I was before I took the class, and reveal Your blessings again to me. Forbid the enemy from blinding me to my growth and the great blessings that come from obedience to You! My heart soars with the opportunity to glorify You!

I might be tempted...to give way to fear...to compare myself to someone else in class...to see my husband in a negative light because he did not respond the way I thought he should...to forget what You have done and are doing...or to minimize Your work in my life. I ask that as I come to this last opportunity in class, where I am to bring glory to Your name by talking about the changes You've made in me, that You open my eyes and help me claim victory! How am I different than before? Show me, I'm listening.

Make me strong in You, Lord, and in Your mighty power! Place on me the full armor of You, so I can take my stand against the enemy's schemes. Help me remember that my struggle is not against flesh and blood, but against the rulers, against the authorities, against the powers of this dark world and against the spiritual forces of evil in the heavenly realms. With Your help, I can stand firm, with the belt of truth buckled around my waist, with the breastplate of righteousness in place, and with my feet fitted with the readiness that comes from the gospel of peace. In addition to all this, help me take up the shield of faith, with which I can extinguish all the flaming arrows of the evil one. I take the helmet of salvation and the sword of the Spirit, which is the Word of God. Help me pray in the Spirit on all occasions, with all kinds of prayers and requests, keep me alert and praying for all the saints, especially my husband and family. Whatever I pay attention to grows – help me focus on YOU!

Remind me once again that it was never my husband's behavior I have sought to change, but rather my own heart and walk with You that will forever need growth. Protect me from any seeds of jealousy the enemy might try to sow in me, and show me what is good, noble, right, pure, lovely, admirable, excellent and praiseworthy in all situations! Keep my eyes turned upon Jesus!

Thank You, for Jesus, for the war being won, thank You for Your protection! May I glorify You with my life, may You make me brave for Your glory, may my life's song sing to You and make You smile…in Christ Jesus, Amen

The wise woman builds her house, but the foolish tears it down with her own hands.
~Proverbs 14:1

I can do all things through Him who gives me strength. ~*Philippians 4:13*

Who can find a virtuous wife? For her worth is far above rubies. ~**Proverbs** *31:10*

We trust that you have connected with God in an intimate way as you have focused on your marriage. As you think back through your journey, we encourage you to take a few moments to write your own prayer, thanking God for what He is doing in your life, recognizing how far He has brought you.

_____
_____
_____
_____
_____
_____
_____
_____
_____
_____
_____
_____
_____
_____
_____
_____
_____
_____
_____
_____
_____
_____
_____
_____
_____
_____
_____

Thank you so much for choosing to step out in faith and take this journey with us! Many women have asked, "What next?" We have several suggestions:

- Gather in small groups with women who were with you on this journey. Continue working on different Steps of Faith and complete another Redeeming Work Journal. Or, set up a time to do the class again with a different focus, maybe even with another group of women.

- Visit the website at: www.GreaterImpact.org and see what is new!

- Complete The Respect Dare® with a group of friends – it's a 40 day devotional experience based on the Daughters of Sarah® course, with an e-course available periodically. This is an easy thing to do with a group. You can do this with our online community or with your church. Find out more at www.GreaterImpact.org .

- Perhaps you are feeling led to be a Titus woman by volunteering your talents to minister to other women – please speak with us!

Whatever you choose to do, know that choosing to do nothing is also a choice--one that the enemy of our souls would have you embrace. Continue to grow and move forward in your walk with God, refusing to be lukewarm.

But in all these things, we overwhelmingly conquer through Him who loved us. For I am convinced that neither death, nor life, nor angels, nor principalities, nor things present, nor things to come, nor powers, nor height, nor depth, nor any other created thing, will be able to separate us from the love of God, which is in Christ Jesus, our Lord.
~Romans 8:37-39

Made in the USA
Middletown, DE
08 November 2014